Hogan How To: Ben Hogan's Five Lessons Distilled

by K. Zachary Haslem

Acknowledgments

This short list of people who have influenced my golf game in paternal ways excludes the golfers who impressed me with their games and instruction, without knowing who I was. That list includes Ben Hogan, Annika Sörenstam, David Duval, Sir Nick Faldo, Butch Harmon, Larry Nelson, Tiger Woods, David Leadbetter, Tom Lehman, Fred Couples, Phil Mickelson, and Corey Pavin. I may have left some out. I'll remember later. They are the people from my impressionable period. The time in a golfer's life when they are becoming inspired. Currently, I'm inspired by Collin Morikawa and Jon Rahm.

The people I've known, who are no less influential, are the ones I actually acknowledge with credit for making this book a reality. My Dad, Rick Haslem, who instilled the values and love of the game that has carried me through long after others would have quit. My late brother, Harley Haslem, for being all the things only a brother can be. Not least of which was my first golfing partner.

PGA Professional Joe Cullinane Jr., for giving me the best first job a boy can have. Picking the range at night, in exchange for an hourly wage and a bucket of balls, per day. Plus permission to pick that bucket up and hit it as many times as I wanted. The clubs I played during those six years with Joe as my pro are so worn the stickers on the shafts have gone long past legible. They're practically embedded into the metal. Had things turned out differently, our six years would have extended into something greater.

More recently, Brian Logsdon and Rob Little. Brian for acknowledging that golf was central to me. In large ways only Brian could make look small. Rob for sharing a burning desire within himself, he'd always eluded to, in such a way as to inspire myself and others.

These are my paternal influences. May we all have them, in golf and in life.

Tiger Woods said Ben Hogan was one of only two golfers to ever own his swing.

Preface

I count the greatest shot I ever hit, not for where it landed, but for where it flew. For one moment in time the ball rose above the moon, so full and blue in the Nevada sky. It floated above the crisp upper rim. All else was dark save but for my target orb, and I would be exiting over the fence as I had many times before. For no golf pro, no matter their patience, could wait till I had my fill of the game.

Foreword

A keer is a time or a turn in Dutch. My first name keern is a dialectic variation on the Dutch word, which means to turn on time. Turning on time is the thing good golfers do best. Golfing icon and multiple major winner William Ben Hogan figured out why the turn was so instrumental to a good golf swing and how to release the club correctly. He got so good at timing his turn and releasing the club correctly, they say he would play out of the same divot all four days of a golf tournament.

Table of Contents

About the author

Prologue

In this book, readers will learn how to incorporate Mr. Hogan's fundamentals into their golf swing using an elegant, repeatable rehearsal motion. This motion was arrived at by overlaying illustrator, Anthony Ravielli's sketches on top of his other sketches throughout *Five Lessons*. I painstakingly traced them over many months. All the while ingraining the information into my own swing. In doing so, I was able to peel back the communication between Mr. Hogan and Ravielli. What I found astounded me. Mr. Hogan had said, "it was all in Five Lessons." Indeed, it was, he had uncovered, in Anthony Ravielli a disciple unlike any other. A man so capable of illustrating the composition and actions of the body, as instructed by golf's most veracious practitioner, that his secret would be hidden in plain sight.

This drill can be used every time a shot is played. Even on pitches and chips. Or it can be used solely in practice. The positions in the drill are critical and should be ingrained in the swing deliberately. The layout of this book will follow Ben Hogan's *Five Lessons: The Modern Fundamentals of Golf* in reverse order. We will begin with the new information introduced in the final chapter of *Five Lessons,* then work our way forward. Incorporating the steps as we go. We will arrive at the true conclusion of *Five Lessons* when we have worked our way back to the first illustration in the body of the book.

Illustrations which overlay various information from *Five Lessons* will be shown. The original illustrations will be cited by page number. Please thumb through your copy of *Five Lessons* to the illustrations being referenced. Although much will be gained from reading *Hogan How To: Ben Hogan's Five Lessons Distilled* on its own, the greatest gains will come from studying the comparisons to *Ben Hogan's Five Lessons: The Modern Fundamentals of Golf.*

Before we delve into the masterwork that is *Five Lessons,* we must establish why. That means setting a goal. For me, the goal is professional level golf at the age of 50. I am currently 47. I started relearning the game left-handed fourteen years ago, in 2012. Two years after accepting the effects of a severe ligament tear. Along the way, I have been very deliberate in my understanding of each motion. Developing not just better ball striking but also an understanding of what wasn't going well, how it felt, and the process behind correcting the flaw. As a natural right-hander, much of what I learned involves how to incorporate the "trail" hand into the golf swing.

In my experience with golf instruction and learning to play the game at a young age, I have found the vast majority of methods come from golfers who had natural ability to begin with. Some if not much of what I describe will appear to be second nature to those of you who have that natural ability. Think of what it feels like to step into the batter's box and visualize the holes (empty places on the field) you could hit. To a natural athlete, this assignment comes easily. The muscles spring to life and anticipation is all that's next. Only the ball need be keyed on for the life in those muscles to fire.

To a new or struggling golfer, the act of delivering the club to the ball is a foreign, painstaking motion. Young people have vast amounts of energy and immeasurable expectations. They *will* athletic actions into being. Golf is such a challenge though that even the young must turn to instruction. Understanding the methods of the game requires a lifelong pursuit. Our mission is to create a golf swing out of building blocks. Our swings will become structurally sound features of our existence. Even as our muscles atrophy and our synapsis conjoin, we will be able to rely on the golf swings we have constructed. Declining strength and mental tenuity will limit us, but in ways we will be able to overcome.

What is your goal? State it clearly and loudly at this moment. Write it in the space below this caption. Digitally or in glorious handwriting. Hear the scrawl of permanence imprint on this page. (A powerful metric for measuring improvement can be found in the addendum of this book.)

Your quest has begun. You will triumph. You will win the prize or conquer the obstacle. Furthermore, you are the golfer you esteem to be. The prize is within your grasp. The celebration is on the horizon.

Chapter 1

Plane ol' Alignment

In the fifth chapter of *Five Lessons* "Summary and Review" three distinct new pieces of information are given. The text reads like a continuation of the previous four chapters. However, the images include details which hadn't been revealed before.

Page 121 puts the waggle into fresh perspective. The Hogan waggle may seam like an antiquated notion. Or a mere tick of the golfer's swing. His waggle served a far greater purpose, though. The accompanying caption in *Five Lessons* describes the benefit of the Hogan waggle, "the golfer actually gets on backswing plane." That key component is experienced through two sensory feedbacks. A) the touching of the right elbow to the hip (he said pocket, but to most of us it will touch well above) and B) the feel of the muscles in the lead hand. That feel is described in anatomical detail in the first chapter of the book.

The first chapter also describes the grip. As well as in the fifth chapter, on pages 116 and 117. Where the outlying aspects of the grip are drawn. As are the locations of calluses. Get used to those specific spots where the hands meet the club. They offer critical feedback for the correct address position. We cannot check everything visually. The grip relies heavily on feel. A good grip is so specific as to rely on tiny callus points throughout the palm and fingers.

The muscles in the lead hand also offer key insights into Hogan's most controversial piece of advice. More on that later.

At first glance, the instructions seam straightforward. Until we attempt to touch our trail elbow to our hip pocket. It turns out the degrees of flexibility required to close that space, without moving our hips, are prohibitive. Rather than give up, do what Hogan instructs, make sure your hip (actually above the hip for those of us with long torsos) touches your elbow. This movement of the hips forward is an excellent rehearsal for the rest of the swing. As in the image, waggle well back of what we see Hogan do in videos. (Because after all, Hogan did many things to conceal his secret, not least of which was to hide it in the images from his book.)

Left-handed at shaft parallel to ground and stance

Right-handed at shaft parallel to ground and stance

Looking down, check to see that the shaft parallels the stance. As with the image in the circle, on page 121. From here, only an on-plane swing can be executed. This drill is not new to the golfing world. One of the great on-plane swingers of all-time, Sir Nick Faldo, has shared this secret widely. For us, it is the foundational building block of a rehearsal motion that unlocks the strongest attribute of a great golf swing.

Now that you've felt the connection point of the dominant arm and the body, you're perfectly positioned to achieve backswing mastery. First, let's delve into the muscles that will be called upon to execute this position, repeatedly.

The muscles in the lead hand as seen on page 21 of *Five Lessons* will get a workout. When you put the club in the stance parallel position the weight rests heavily on those muscles running through the hand from wrist to knuckles. This feeling is an important one. It will repeat, in the Hogan swing, in three key positions.

Play for at least three weeks while deliberately using this waggle. Not only are you training your swing to get on plane, you're also strengthening those all essential muscles. In fact, you likely will feel those muscles flex at impact. That is, if your grip is correct. Reference *Five Lessons* for detailed instruction.

Before taking a shot, first execute the waggle, experience the parallels of the shaft with the stance. It will even feel as though your alignment is being established by this position. To check, pause at the top of the back waggle, with the shaft parallel to the stance. Those muscles in your lead hand will be flexed. While the shaft is paused parallel to the stance, swivel (not tilt) your head toward the target. Looking down the eye-line at the target, you'll notice your shaft is also pointed there.

The back of your lead wrist should be flattened. As we see on close inspection of the image from Chapter 5. That position precisely describes impact. Hence, your flexed lead hand muscles at the top of the waggle will repeat at impact. This connection of the lead hand muscles to the club and club face is critical to good ball striking.

Hogan advised using the shadow to inform our practice

We are about to see this same angle in the third chapter. It is Hogan's Angle, and it unlocks his secret.

This distant side of the ball in line with our dominant arm is referred to as Hogan's Angle. It informs the function of that dominant arm both now and in the through swing.

We will explore how the club shaft, which is put on plane through this alignment drill, travels in an arc. While the club face is controlled through a continuum of Hogan's Angle. This synchronization of the body turn with our natural inclination to use our dominant arm diagonally, across from us, is how the golf ball can be struck well, repeatably.

Gravity Fall

We turn the page of *Five Lessons* to 122. Where we see two new pieces of information displayed in tandem. In earlier chapters, the idea of the hips and shoulders as ovals was introduced. In this image, the hips and shoulders are joined by an arrow and a dot. There is also an omission, around the hands, in the shading of the position at impact, which is meant to demonstrate the position of the hands. As seen on the page below. Except, unlike the below image, the hands are not in the center of the circle.

These two new pieces of information describe the center of the swing. To feel this center, we will employ the next step in our drill. From the previous position, with the shaft parallel to the ground, and the stance, permit the club to drop. However, do not let the club face pass square.

You'll notice when gravity takes hold the club head *does not* fall to the back of the ball. It descends, then rolls into a slot which is above the ball. This aspect of the plane is depicted on page 88 of Five Lessons. In fact, it takes effort to force the club head downward. This effort is what plagues many golfers. The act of forcing the club down to the back of the ball creates slices, chunks and mis-hits.

Note: if the club head falls to the back of the ball, without turning the club face past square, your golf grip is not correct.

Why does the golf club rise when it is not allowed to close over? That has to do with the angle of the club through your hands. That angle establishes a core fundamental of the golf swing. The center of the swing.

The center of the swing is the space between the butt of the club and the body at address. The center of the swing should not be violated throughout the critical movements of the swing. Only after impact, when the body is recoiling into a resting position, should the swing's center be occupied by any part.

In these next paragraphs, we will explore one of the ways Hogan paired with his illustrator, Anthony Ravielli, to conceal Ben Hogan's Secret within the pages of *Five Lessons*. This *DaVinci Code* level uncovering is a joy to behold.

First, let us consider the arrow in the oval. The arrow clearly denotes the front of the hips, at approximately the location of the belt buckle. (Hogan wore his trousers incredibly high. As we saw with the right elbow to the hip pocket instruction for the waggle.) We see that location tie in with the hands in the illustration on pages 94 and 95. That tie-in leads us to the next question. What does the dot denote?

Where in the golf swing do we see a black dot small enough to occupy the top of the shoulder but big enough to cover the bone bump? A dot approximately the size of a quarter dollar. Let us begin with the illustration on page 47. Since the dot in the ovals references a point in the shoulder, it stands to reason that illustrations comprised around the lead shoulder would inform us as to the bearing of that dot.

If we have not already surmised the relevance of the black dot let us turn the pages further toward the front of the book. Where we do not see a black dot until page 23. Loe and behold, for some reason there is just one. Just one in a sea of possible black dots, among all the illustrations we have passed. And that one black dot is being held not by both hands but just one. One hand as it is illustrated in connection with the whole body. The adjacent image, which omits the black dot, only depicts the hand. The one with the blackened butt-end of the golf club is shown along with the arm. As it is connected to Mr. Hogan's body. Precisely as we would expect from the illustration of Hogan standing erect, with only his lead arm on the club, on page 47. The black dot is connected through the body at the shoulder. The butt of the club and the left shoulder have a union. And now we know what the arrow and black dot inside the ovals from chapter 5 are. Clues to the center of the golf swing.

I have already stated the precise location of the center of the golf swing. That is no mystery. But what of its relevance. We can accept that the center of the golf swing must not be invaded until after impact. Still images from good golf swings show this to be true.

Hogan showed us how the center of the golf swing remains unmoved. In the series from page 122. Hence, out of position with the hands, after the arc has moved him forward in the downswing.

We feel in our exercise the effect of the center of the swing. As it refuses to permit a natural motion which removes the club from their connection. Next we will exercise the large body action, on the opposite hemisphere of center, whereby the golf club arrives at the back of the ball, repeatedly and with remarkable consistency.

We see in the shadow the way the hands hold the club aloft.

Feel, as you attain this position, the retention of the grip inside the hands.

Chapter 2

Centrifugal Force

In the gravity-driven descent of the club, the position of the hands dictate the club will swing out and above the ball. The club likely will have come to rest in the air above the ball. With the shaft in line with the placement of the ball, relative to the stance. Ideally, above the ball and inside the lead foot.

We turn to page 125, where we see a diagram. As with the previous illustrations sited from Chapter 5, this illustration provides new information.

As we have seen from our descent exercise, gravity determines the placement of the ball. Gravity, as it connects to the lead arm, which is gripping the shaft at its longest point. That *is not* the bottom of the swing.

We are about to see how to enact the forces which drive the club beyond gravity, through with speed to the bottom of the swing, and on to the follow through.

Up to this point, your feet may well have been parallel to one another, perpendicular to the target line. Your feet may have been making a square, more or less, or rectangle. Alternatively, they may have been sloppily splayed outward. Let us consider why that is not ideal.

On page 125 we see foot positioning, throughout the bag. On page 42 the positioning of the front foot is given in exacting detail. A one quarter rotation of the front foot provides a measurement of the bottom of the swing.

These next motions will take your rehearsal from the position of the ball to the bottom of the swing. They will incorporate correct body movement and weight shift into your understanding of the golf swing.

The below illustration is taken from page 125 and layered, to depict the rotation of the body and weight shift. From beyond impact and into the bottom of the swing.

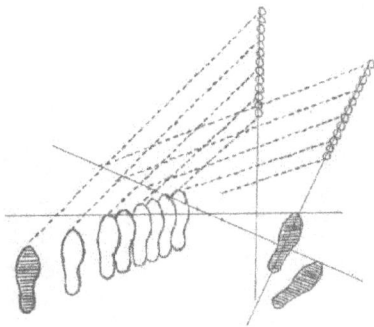

Left-handed address position to bottom of the swing

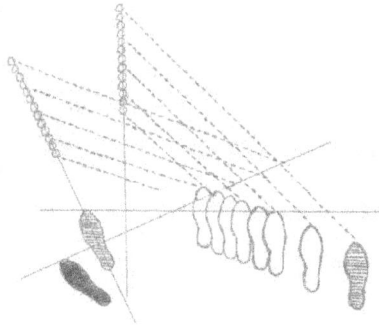

Right-handed address position to bottom of the swing

Note the shaded foot in the right-handed version. That weight shift away from center is one of the prevailing things professionals do that amateurs do not. Their weight moves away from center. Amateurs violate center with their hands and hips. In the previous chapter, we talked about forcing the club head down to the ball. That effort of the hands should not happen.

Instead, the hips must move away from center. The way to rehearse this feeling is to first turn the front foot one quarter turn out. Next, understand that your intentions must bear to a direction which is perpendicular to that foot. See how the lines intersect in the center of the foot?

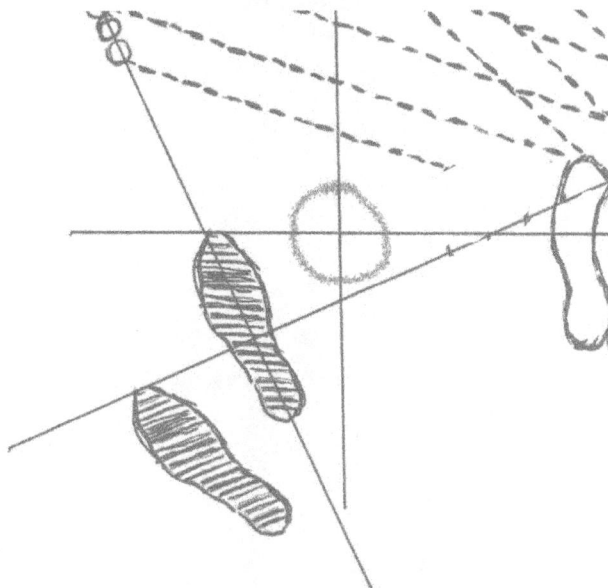

The circle is from chapter 1. The center of the swing, as shown at address. In the through swing our weight moves away from center.

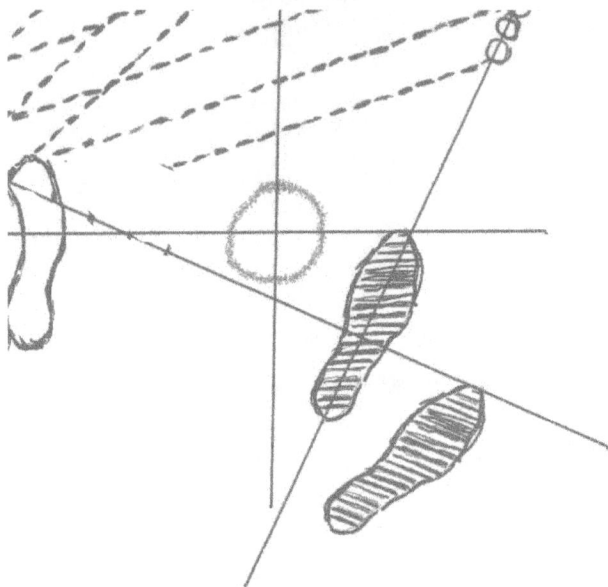

Shown here is the left handed version.

On page 99 of *Five Lessons*, we see one of Hogan's most misunderstood pieces of instruction. The old two-handed basketball pass. At first glance, the two-handed basketball pass is simply made down the line, at the target. Further inspection reveals this cannot be the case.

Resume your rehearsal motion. This time take the club back to first position, the position from plane ol' alignment. Next, accelerate the club beyond gravity fall to directly above the front foot. Let the club follow the same inside out and upward path. So that the club is actually quite far above the ground. When you look down through it, your foot and the club should be directly in line. Just like we see in the illustration, with the balls out ahead of the foot.

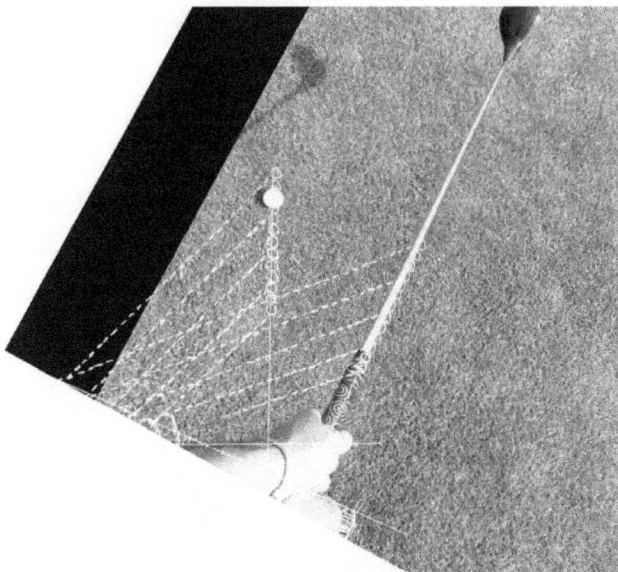

Club over and in line with front foot

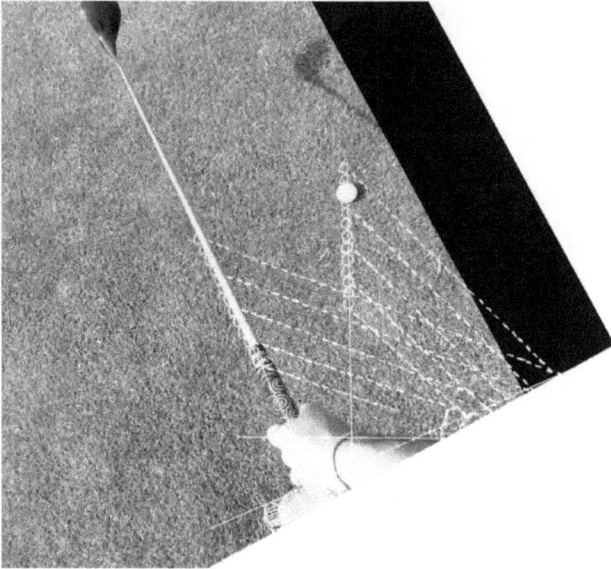

Weight moves back onto left hip. Over the intersection of the lines in the middle of the foot.

The confusion over the images on page 99 is understandable. The images on the bottom half of the page show the golf swing going down the line. The basketball pass image does not, however, show the lower body. For the lower body to work as it should, the hands must be intent on that line which is perpendicular to the front foot. In a basketball game, the pass would be made to a player who was to the passers side, but without opening the stance. The throw would be over the front foot. Not from the chest, which is the norm. Rather around the front of the body.

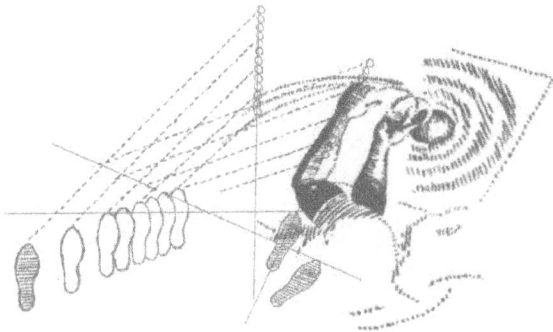

The reason the basketball target is perpendicular to our front
foot is simple. The hands separate. Our dominant hand
continues down the line.

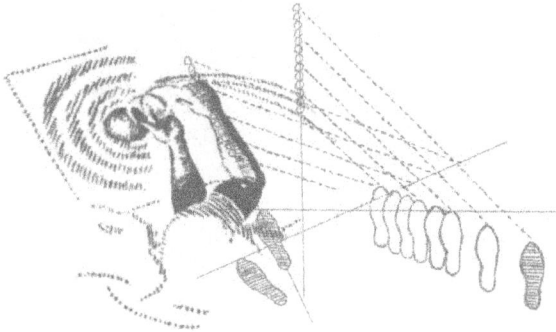

The dominant hand follows the target line only with the bullseye far to the left. We will see more about where exactly the bullseye is located. Hogan described its proximity in detail.

Author at address

In plane parallel position

Club over front foot looking four to five yards down eyeline

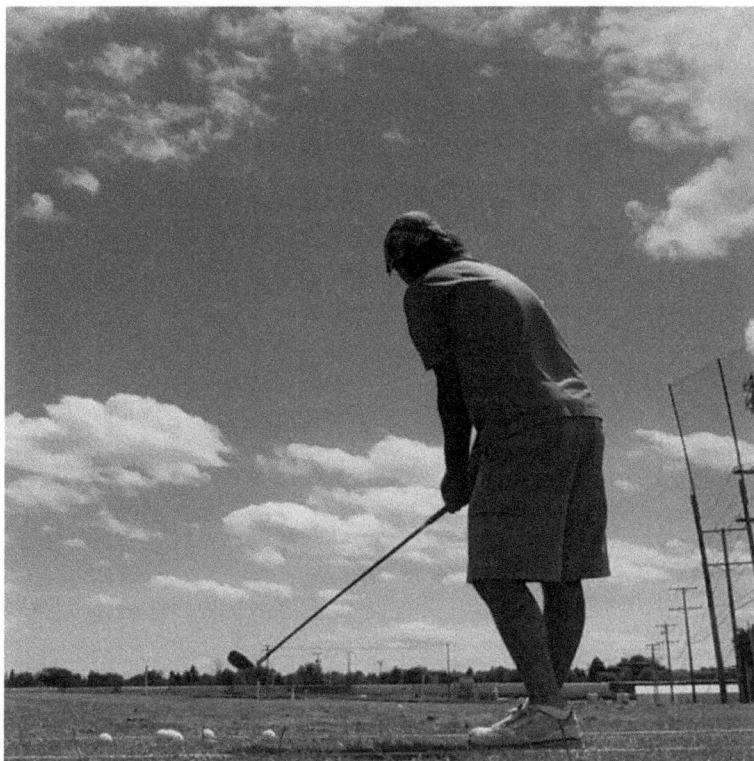

Now planning the shot, while keeping body in two handed pass position

We know it is advisable for the club in our rehearsal motion to be well above the ground because Hogan advocates for a motion which is not downward. Rather he instructs us to hit a target which is about the height of the belt buckle (his being quite high as we've discussed.) With your club above your foot, in line with the balls in the illustration, look to a point four or five yards well ahead, to where the club face is pointing. For right-handed golfers, this direction is well left of the target line—perpendicular to your front foot—and note the feel of your weight moving correctly. Away from center and over your front heel. At full speed, your weight will try to displace your foot, into the position shown in the shaded version of the illustration.

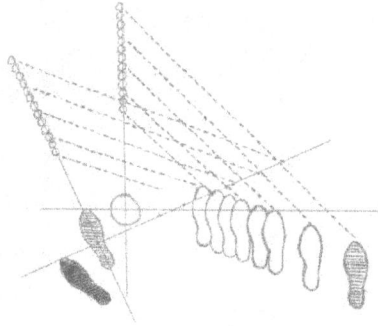

A note on the inclusion of left and right-handed illustrations. It wasn't until I had to relearn the game left-handed that I was able to break down the necessary aspects of the golf swing. Like many players who took up the game at a young age, I did not fully understand what I was doing. Indeed, many teaching pros cannot identify with the struggles of golfers who take up the game in their adult years. This occurs because their learning process took place before their conscious mind could get in the way. They learned, as I had, how to hit the ball through repetition and unconscious action.

Hogan knew he could not become the player he wanted to be by relying solely on his natural abilities. He had to break the swing down into repeatable axioms. Which is why his descriptions uphold such an exacting standard.

In the coming chapters, we will fully elaborate on the release and the flight of the ball, as it pertains to this moment. Whereby the ball has been struck prior to our current position. What we have described up to this moment is a path the club takes, which is outward and above the ball. The weight shift away from this outward path causes the club and ball to meet, and the ball travels up a line which is midway between.

Seen here is a simple sketch of a golfer, the center of the swing, and how Hogan instructed Ravielli to place the center of the swing at an intersection in the stance.

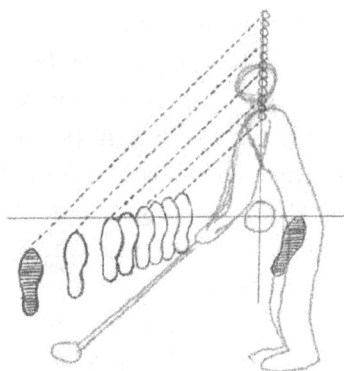

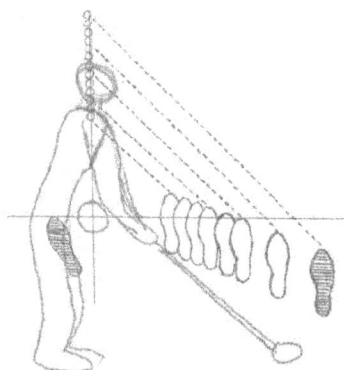

Chapter 3

The Elusive *Correct* Release

Even good players struggle to connect their hip action with their hand action. They know, like all of us, that the hips must flash hard laterally and turn. The act of putting the club to the ball is somehow so often separate, though. That is why so few golfers have mastered the one shape shot. And those who do score better.

The hallmark of a good golfer who struggles with shot shape is "on days." Some days are superb. The timing is just there. An unconscious connection of hands and hips.

This happens because the feedback we receive at address is not the same as impact. From our address position, we receive information that is parallel to us. At impact, we have turned to equally between parallel and perpendicular.

Hogan could provide himself with the correct information with a subtle waggle. The subtlety of the waggle he used in competition is not the same as the waggle in his summary chapter. The image on page 121, which describes plane alignment, is better for golfers who don't practice daily, as Hogan did.

In addition to an amateur level waggle, he provided everything we need to know to rehearse the impact position and correctly inform ourselves on the release.

If you've been executing the rehearsal motions, as they've been presented, you will have gained a feel for timing. We see timing in the direction of our club face at the turning point. Hogan also parsed out an impediment which keeps timing from being automatic. In your rehearsal motion, you may have noticed the thumb and forefinger of your dominant hand holding the club aloft at the turning point.

The turning point in the golf swing.

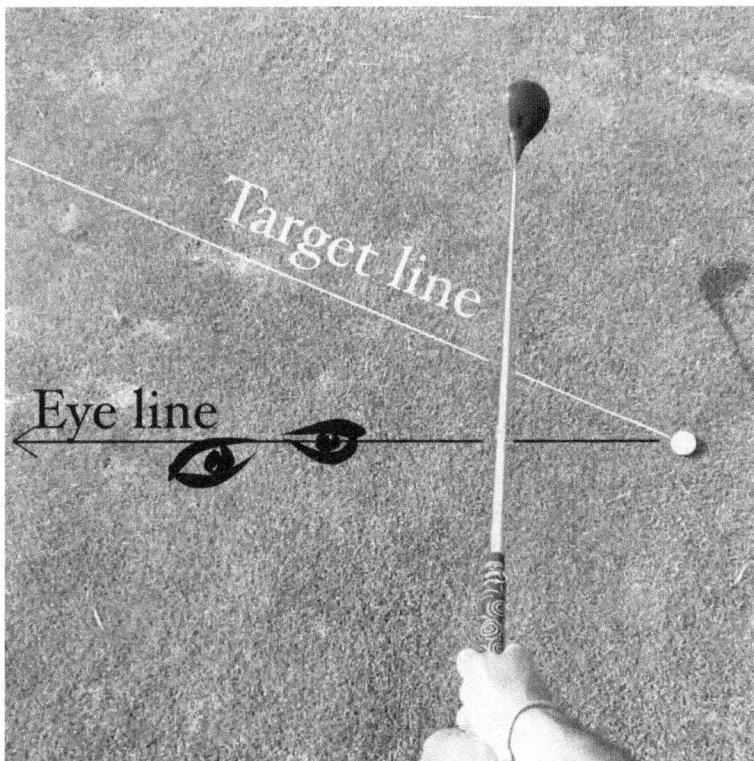

On page 97 of *Five Lessons*, we see the release being compared to a sidearm throw in baseball. The important thing here, as illustrated with bold lines, is the relationship between these fingers and the arm and body. The text describes how tension between the thumb and forefinger will cause tension up the arm and into the shoulder.

On page 31 we see how to experience the feeling of this release with the golf club in our hands. We do so by pointing our thumb and forefinger in the shape of an L. We should make our release prior to the turning point.

In doing so, we put the weight of the club in the other fingers of the hands. Instead of relying on our pincers for face control, we are syncing our body rotation with the club face. Hogan could not over-stress the importance of body/arm connection.

He elaborated on the direction of the elbows, as they relate to the hips, on pages 49, 50 and 51. Then went on to illustrate, along with Anthony Ravielli, the interconnectedness of the muscles throughout the chest, legs, shoulders, and arms on page 58. We see so little to do with arm swing until the release. The backswing and downswing are executed with the turning of the hips and shoulders.

The arm swing is the uncontrollable aspect of most golf swings. One day, the arms separate from the body by inches, the next half as much. The golfer then complains that their swing feels "off," compared to before. The very same function that initiates a good release also controls the degree of arm swing, though. And that is the action of the dominant arm.

Notice in the above images how the dominant arm, the release arm, parallels the target line. This point, the turning point in the golf swing, is the moment of truth. Hogan said the moment of greatest swing speed occurred a foot or two after the ball. I'm guessing he provided measurements for both tall and short golfers. Or in my case, high ball hitters (left-handed) and medium trajectory hitters (right handed.) Correctly believing that golfers of any height would experience that moment somewhere between a foot and two after the ball. (Hogan also accounted for tall golfers on page 80, in his description of the plane.) Flat does not equate to Hogan. Plane equates to Hogan.

Engaging the dominant arm establishes plane. A person's natural throwing motion will have a huge effect on *their* plane. My left-handed throwing motion is closer to my body and lower than my right-handed throwing motion. My left-handed swing is tighter and flatter. Importantly, it's consistent with my (albeit learned) nature.

The lead arm in the right-handed swing has separated from the body. Flailing will result in the following stills.

The lead wrist has cupped, opening the club face and engaging
the muscles from page 23.

Being this loaded on the back leg, left-handed, will certainly send the ball sky high.

We see here knee flex in the left-handed swing. Hogan advised stabilizing the back hip against a golf club, on page 75. There is a surprising amount of shoulder turn against a restricted hip.

In these stills the club seams destined to release at the camera.

The lag in the left-handed swing is held longer because the tendons and ligaments in the right arm are intact. Able to contribute.

This early lunge off the right heal (right-handed) is a consistency killer.

In this image we see the reason I play left handed. My left arm is missing a ligament (2007) and a tendon (2024). For those reasons I cannot maintain a bowed wrist through impact in my right-handed swing.

This left handed swing enjoys the benefit of much more work with our rehearsal motion. Whereas the right-handed swing still suffers carryovers, such as the lifted right heal, from insufficient understanding.

The left hand just doesn't speed through the left-handed swing like the right hand does in the right-handed swing. Indeed, it can barely keep up.

Left-handed the shot was a slight two yard fade down the center of the fairway. Right-handed the ball drew into the left rough. A long scorcher of a golf shot. Into thick grass.

If you have a question about the right plane for you, (are you an upright or flat swinger of the golf club), simply put your dominant elbow in its natural throwing position. Believe it or not, a raised elbow could be right for you.

Hogan's illustrations of plane demonstrate how the dominant arm facilitates good plane. On page 88 the downswing plane can only be caused to change by the initiation of the dominant arm. We see an embarrassing error in this particular drawing. The illustrator did not use one point perspective. Instead, Anthony Ravielli followed Mr. Hogan's instruction. The arrows illustrating the backswing and downswing plane point up, not away. Every illustrator since the sixteenth century has learned how to draw one-point perspective. By artist standards, the arrow lines should start out fat and get thin as they go away. They would, were it not for Hogan. Insisting that the arrows should illustrate the under and upward motion of the right arm.

That two plane image depicts the very same motion that puts our rehearsal in the turning point position, with the club above the ball, and moving outward.

Let us pause for a moment to consider the ramifications of this suggestion. For how long now has "hitting down" been the mantra of golfers? We must hit down for the ball to go up. Yes, that is true. The club descends, and the ball ascends. The club descends because of its connection to our *non-dominant* (lead) arm. Hogan shows us this on pages 102 and 103. On those pages, the supination, or bowing of the lead wrist, is shown in tandem with the correct arc. The arc being one circle on the backswing and an advanced circle on the downswing.

This left-handed POV shows the club shaft staying in line with the lead arm through impact. Producing great consistency.

This right-handed POV shows the shaft passing the lead hand, shortly after impact. This creates lack of consistency. However the right arm is in a great release position. More work with the rehearsal would cut down on the amount of right leg action too.

The arc of the golf swing is determined by the lead arm.

Many golfers take this motion to great lengths. Their arm swing becomes the source of their distance. The greater the arc, the greater the distance. The key to consistency, they suppose, is a radically advanced shaft angle—shaft lean—at impact. Here is the question, and the rub against this way of thinking, "when does the dominant arm apply force?" Almost all of us have them, and they are insistent.

Chapter 4

The Rehearsal Motion

First, take your stance. The shoulders and insteps of the feet are interconnected. The illustration on page 125 shows the foot placement for all clubs throughout the bag. With one critical back foot position. The singular foot in the middle of them all, with none touching on either side. That is the stance width of a long iron. On page 41 that stance width is said to be for the five iron. The insteps are shoulder width apart. The driver and woods are wider-than and the mid, short iron and wedges are narrower.

Hogan was thorough in his description of the front foot quarter turn, as shown on page 42, for very good reason. In taking your stance, make sure that position is exact. The back foot must be square, to restrict the back swing. The front foot must be quartered out. To create a precise measurement for the key moment in the golf swing and turning point of the hips.

Know your grip by its calluses. Pages 116 and 117 reiterate this. Feel the grip in your hands by those pressure points. *Know* them. Find that feeling each time you hold the club. We address the club face, at the back of the ball.

However, we know from Hogan, our orientation to center is the most critical. The lead arm must be stationed at center. As shown in the stance diagram, from page 125. The center of the swing and the middle of the stance are not the same. The intersection of those lines is at the center of the golf swing. If the ball is positioned behind center, impact will occur early. If the ball is ahead of center, impact will occur late. Shaft angle will be affected. More on this in Chapter 5.

A draw is unlikely with the Hogan methods because timing is established through body rotation and draws occur by releasing the hands before the body.

The fluidity of the following motions depends upon one's natural cadence and familiarity with the exercise. Except for the turning point, these motions should be executed with painterly exactitude. While having the lie, trajectory and shot in mind.

Our degree of control over outcomes occurs in the order of lie, trajectory, and shot. We presently situate ourselves to the lie, next we will endeavor to achieve a trajectory, whereby the finish will be the shot. The lie dictates our stance. We know the position of the ball, according to Hogan's diagram. The ball may be above or below our feet or on an uphill or downhill lie. These factors alter the position of our grip on the club, e.g., choked up for a stance which is below the ball. The trajectory is a factor of club choice and efforts at impact. Those efforts are rehearsed with the waggle.

We waggle into the plane ol' alignment position. Having our alignment in mind. We may pause to check the position of the shaft. This is a good time to re-situate our feet. If we feel uncomfortable with what we see out of the corner of our eye.

Our key checkpoints in the back waggle are the touching of the elbow to the hip and the flattening of the lead wrist. This position simulates impact and gets the club on plane. The illustration inside the large circle on page 121 shows the extent to which this motion can go. The feel of the muscles in the lead hand being flexed is an important one. Ravielli illustrated them, and they are included on page 23.

A note on Hogan's most controversial piece of advice, which was not included in Five Lessons. In the Time Magazine article of 1955 he recommended cupping the lead wrist at the top of the backswing. For him, that was a critical factor in his dominant ball striking. Many criticisms of this move have been lodged. For the reason that most amateurs would exaggerate a slice. To Hogan, this motion engaged the same muscles he would use at impact to stabilize the club face. The four tendons in our lead hand that run to our hand bones are left white in the illustration. The waggle, the cupping of the lead wrist and supination at impact share the sensation of engaging them. Those muscles/tendons provided him with the feedback he needed.

The idea that we swing the club face goes against the instruction Hogan provided. We actually turn our hips to one hemisphere of center and swing our hands and club to the other. Meanwhile, our lead shoulder acts as the axis around which our lead arm pivots. The nucleus being the center of the swing. It is this relationship of the hips, hands, and shoulder assembly with the center of the swing which dictates shot shape and quality. The center of the golf swing, unlike the orbit of the club face, is easily appraised at every juncture.

At the top of the back waggle, we enlarge the space taken up by the center of the golf swing. From there we will move into the turning point. Simultaneously, permitting the club to fall to outside the ball while turning our hips to perpendicular with our front foot. The club now points the same direction as the front foot.

Do not cut this corner. With utmost deliberateness look to a point four or five yards ahead, in line with the quarter turned foot to a place perpendicular to that front foot. This place will be at an acute angle from the target line. The measurement of that angle is one half of 45 or 22 and 1/2 degrees. In the process of making this turn you will establish a posted up front leg, turn of the hips consistent with Hogan's digram from page 122 and correct position of the right elbow. As shown on pages 91, 94 and 95.

There is a natural question of, "how does the club head get down to the ball?" After all, we are rehearsing an above the ball motion. The same kind of above the ball motion shown on pages 91, 94, 95, 97, 99, and back to 31. Where Hogan demonstrates the importance of removing the pincer fingers of the dominant hand (thumb and forefinger) from the grip.

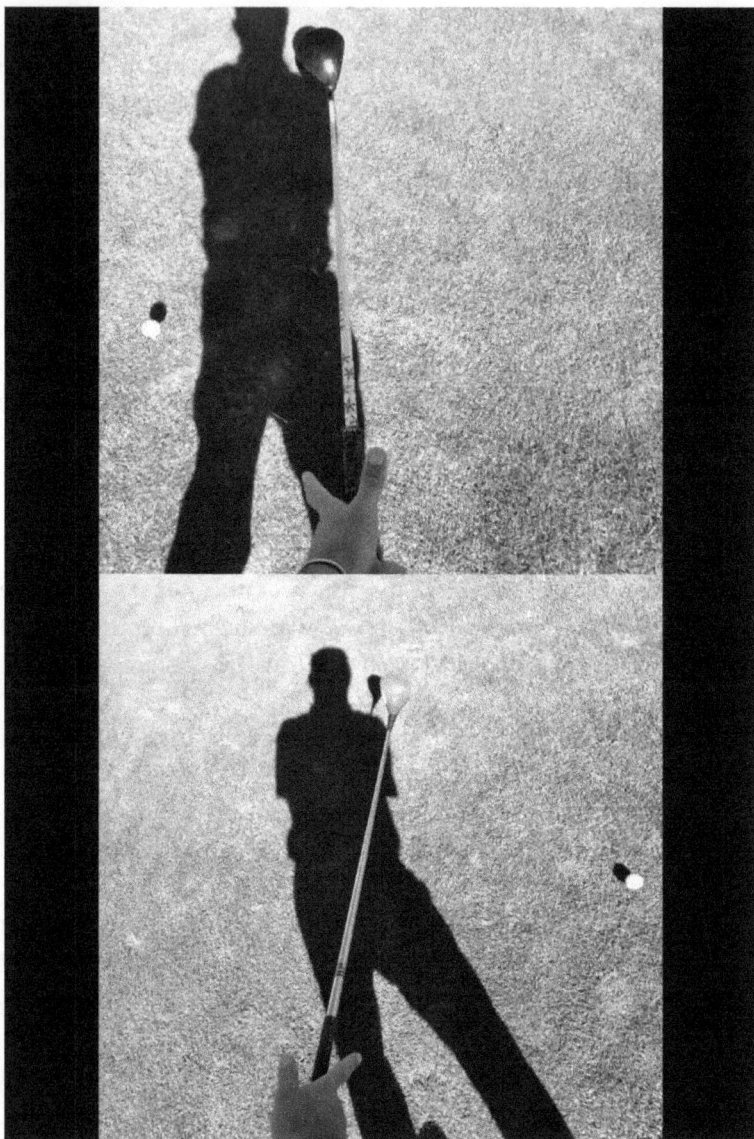

As the club and body approach the turning point, release the club with the thumb and forefinger of your dominant hand. This does not in itself cause the club to drop to the back of the ball. It does put the club in a free swinging motion. Whereby its connection to the body is unimpeded. From this position, having released the club, with our hips and head turned acutely toward the four to five yard mark, the club face matches our hands. Closed evenly to the target line.

We are ready to paint the shot, with our mind. While retaining the positions of our hips, shoulders, arms, and club, we look to the sky. Why to the sky and not the target. Not yet to the target. First to the sky. Because as the ball passes through a point about the height of our belt buckle, it will be on its way into the sky.

Gravity. In a word, how does the club get down to the ball? Gravity. We are about to defy gravity. The club must go down for the ball to go up. There are two pulls of gravity in this equation. There is the earth, and there is the gravity of the center of the golf swing.

When we first experimented with dropping the club from the back waggle position, we learned that the golf grip must give out for the club to fall to the back of the ball. In the absence of a turn of the body, the club can only fall back to the ground if the grip fails. Our golf grip does not fail.

Therefore, our body must defy the gravity of the center of the swing. So that the upward and outward motion of the club will be rerouted to the back of the ball. Our hips and legs will drive down and away. Down and away from the center of the golf swing. They will do this because that is what we have rehearsed. And with our minds trained on launching the ball skyward, our swing will obey.

We cannot envision the golf shot without exploring Hogan's end goal, as depicted in *Five Lessons*. We see it in the first illustration in the body of the book. Not the first illustration that precedes the body. An image of Hogan approaching impact. The first image in the body of the book. Which shows Hogan approaching impact on the right and the substantive qualities of Hogan's swing. As depicted through a combination of electrical motors and circuitry, on the left. This image tells a whole story. A story which we arrived at by working our way from back to front, through the illustrations.

A circumspect notion of the golf swing would perceive the image on the right as if Hogan were hitting the ball down the line.

All things trained on the target. This idea of parallels pervades the imaginations of all golfers. In that construct, the hips and hands fire in parallel. Every bit of energy moving forward, side by side. All things at the target. This notion fails for one radically simple reason, in Newtonian physics. For every action, there is an equal and opposite reaction.

If all things are firing in parallel, at the target, what occurs in opposition? The body's mass moves hard at the target, and the arm assembly chases an arc, down the target line. They both move abreast to the left, for right-handed golfers. Their synchronization depends not on physics, but on a series of mental gymnastics. Performing a feat which sometimes delivers the club face square, hips in perfect union, but more often than not results in shots which move one way or the other. Even in apparently good golf swings, the ball turns hard one way one swing and hard the other the next.

Looking at the electrified image at the left. To the average golfer's mind, the motor in the head is turned perpendicular to the target line, on an axis squarely facing the target. Likewise, the motor in the body is turned perpendicular, squarely affixed on the distant target. The synchro in the hands would be square as well. That notion of square and parallel plagues the game, at every level. Only putting is square.

Hogan saw it differently, and had the differences drawn for us. The generators in the head and body are askew. Their axes point outward. The synchro in the hands demonstrates this overtly. It is far from square. Directed instead at an angle we have already established. Hogan's Angle is away from the direction the motors are turning. Widely away, in fact. So much so it could be said the hands and body are moving in opposite directions. The force behind the club and the movement of the body are equal and opposite. If A the body and B the hands are being pulled down C the line of flight, and they depart obliquely, the distance between them is expanding. They are moving in opposite directions.

Upon closer inspection, we should define the large components in the head and chest as generators. They provide the power to the transistors in the elbows, motors in the hips and a synchro in the hands. There are motors in each hip. Those motors create torque. If you've ever wondered what torque is, pick up a drill. Particularly, an old-fashioned plug in type or cheap drill (they really move) and pull the trigger. Feel the drill twist in your hands. That torque is a directional force caused by the abrupt winding of the motor coil. Hogan's right and left hip wound hard in opposite directions. This is how he kept from falling over. Similarly, his hands followed the path of the right hip. That is why the distance between the right hip and right elbow is closed at impact.

Hogan's major motor coils, the generators in his head and chest, wound hard to the aft, behind his lead side, in the direction we've rehearsed. The same is true of professional golfers. We see this motion when we watch televised golf. However, Hogan did something remarkable, we will cover in Chapter 5. The evidence was in his golf swing and, above all, his book. He defined the precipitous actions better than anyone. In a core way. With imagery.

The feels, though, that professional golfers have, and Hogan has imbued us with, are real. They're most often appraised through natural ability and tens of thousands of golf balls. Or much more readily by executing the rehearsal motion described herein.

What does it feel like? It should feel less like guess work. When you're holding the club aloft, ahead of the ball, over your lead foot, at the turning point, and you've looked four to five yards ahead, in line with your body—perpendicular to your front foot—you've put yourself in max position. From there, the shot is more visible than at address. Quite possibly more so than ever. Looking at the target, foreseeing the shot fly, while holding that pose, (having made a back waggle, to assure good plane) your heart should swell.

Power generation, the kind Hogan had Ravielli illustrate, happens inside your chest. In that domain where all your best efforts resort. That feeling, in conjunction with the power plant within your head, that is what you should feel. Those feelings should be robust. The reason we are doing this, our desire to delve deeply into Mr. Hogan's masterwork, is the strong charge of ability being transferred from within, like a bolt, to the golf ball!

Chapter 5

How does the turn work?

At address, we experience the target as being to the side. That is the only time in the golf swing we are parallel to the target. At impact, our body is turned open to the target, in line with the turn. When we rehearse the turn, we establish a target that is about the height of our belt buckle, four to five yards ahead.

Then we perceive the flight of the ball. We perceive the flight because it will pass through the bullseye, at that height.

In their setup of this illustration Hogan appears to have had
Ravielli position himself so the horizon line of the canvas was

the same as the line from Hogan's front foot. Essentially, Hogan pointed his front foot at Ravielli.

A very good thing happens when we acquaint ourselves with the belt buckle target. We experience the body turn first and then empower our dominant hand to feel as though it is catching the ball from the ground and hurling it through the bullseye.

Hogan famously said, "I found it in the dirt." Consider this expression. There are two places we find the dirt. The divot that remains where the ball *was* and the divot that flies. Both provide evidence. The dirt that flies provides evidence of the flight of the ball. Where do we find that divot? The answer, somewhere beyond and between the two bullseyes in the above image. If there were a bullseye for the divot to hit, that bullseye would also be located approximately four to five yards ahead.

To a man who said, "The ultimate judge of your swing is the flight of the ball." Ben Hogan, which is the greater indicator? The negative of the divot, left behind in the fairway, or the divot that chases the ball? The answer, both. Replacing divots and fixing pitch marks are our most informative acts. Not doing those things is like measuring a heartbeat without a stethoscope.

Remember the Gravity Fall section. From the back waggle position, you were instructed to not let the club face go past square. Try the exercise again, this time *permit* the club face to close as much as it will. This closing over of the club face allows it to descend to the ground.

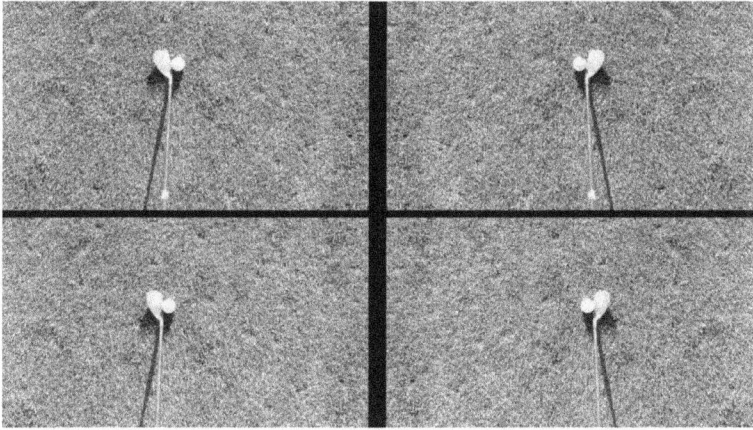

Top R and L: Hogan grip and setup. Bottom: Hogan grip and standard setup.

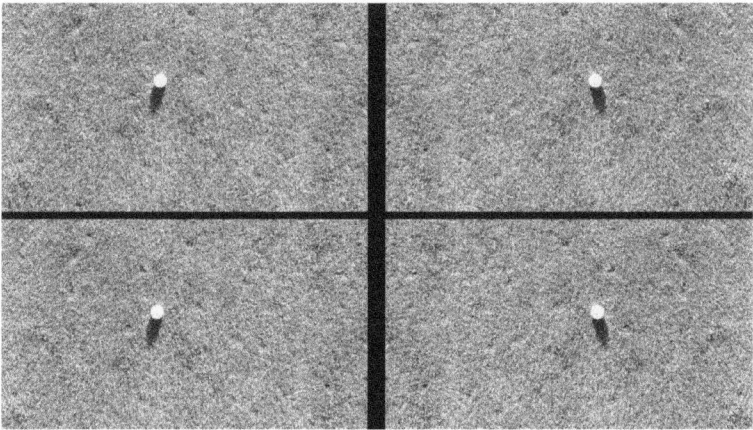

At the top of the back waggle. Club is parallel to stance and target line.

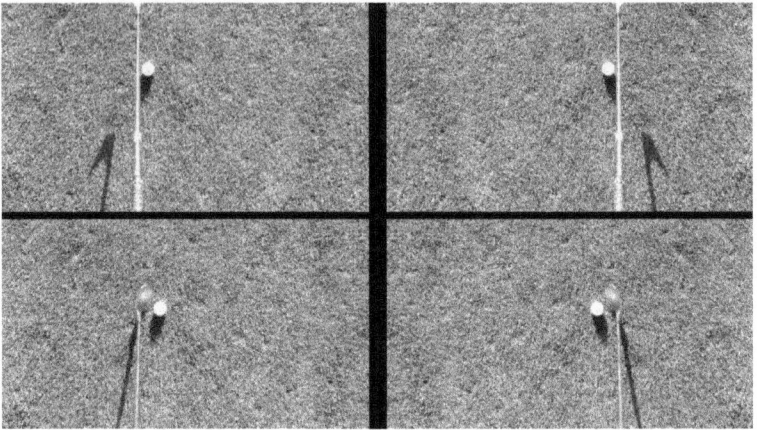

Top: gravity fall down to stance bottom, without letting the face close past square. Bottom: gravity fall to the bottom letting the face turn over.

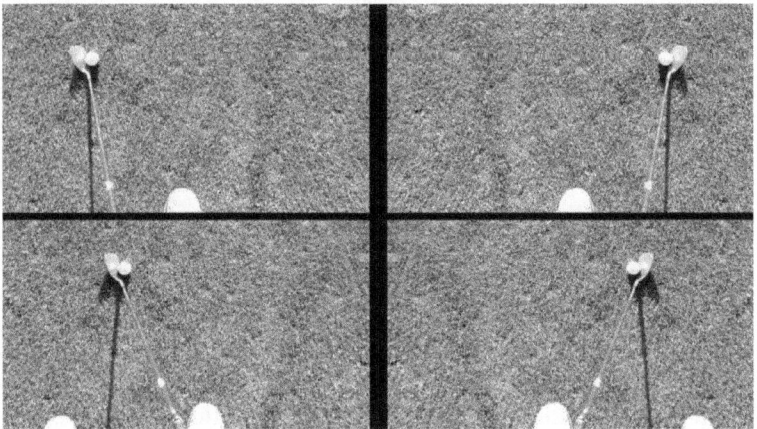

Top: front hip moved away from center, as in rubber band image from page 91, until club has lowered to behind the ball.

Bottom: shaft bent forward until club face is square. Also with hip turn toward target.

Next, as seen in the bottom panels of the above image, lean the closed-over club forward until the club face reaches square. This is the standard approach to the golf swing. In the decades since *Five Lessons* was misunderstood, instructors and the golfing public have accepted this hand position as standard.

"Reverse every natural instinct and do the opposite of what you are inclined to do, and you will probably come very close to having a perfect golf swing." Ben Hogan.

The above panels are arrived at by bringing the club down to the ball, through leaning your weight to the posterior, onto your lead heel. Hogan outlined posture on page 54 as a feeling of sitting on a stadium seat. Such seats aren't in use anymore, but the principle remains the same. This sitting posture is comfortable. Get used to it, in your address. Creating the weight shift to simulate impact is a bit challenging. The feeling can be found on page 91, of the large rubber band pulling Hogan to a wall behind him. You're both sitting back and leaning your weight onto your lead heel. Also allow your trail knee to press in toward the middle. (The reason we do the entire rehearsal motion, not just to above the ball, is it is easier to move our weight over our front heel when we do not force ourselves to stay down.)

Next, follow the experiment as below. Do both the above example and the below. In the above, your body lowered the club to the ball. In the below, your hands lowered the club to the ball, then advanced the shaft to square the club face. See how in the above example, the club face does not deviate from square with the changing of the shaft angle. In the bottom example, though, where the hands lowered the club head to the ball, the shaft deviates along with the shaft lean.

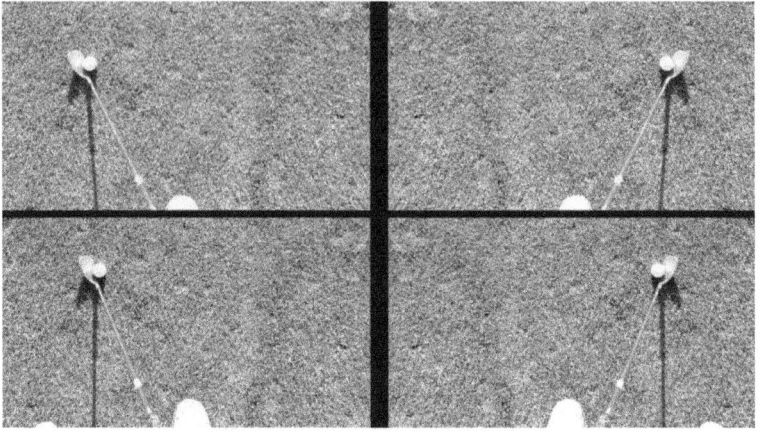

Top: shaft leaned forward to parallel impact position in bottom (standard) image.

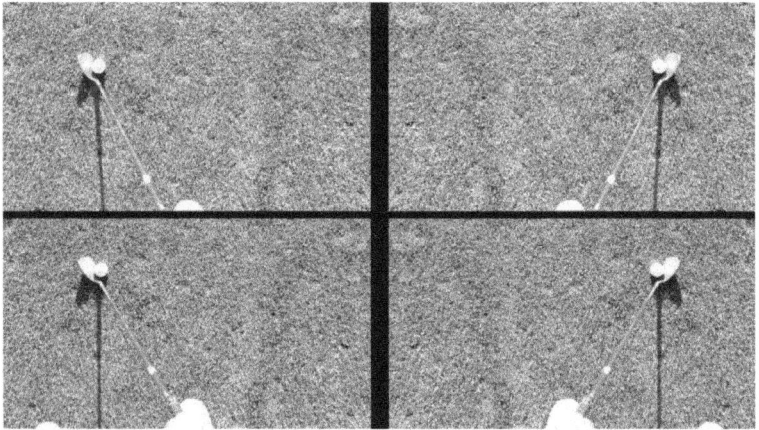

Bottom: shaft moved further forward. Note the club face opens.

Importantly, you're building the muscle memory of a neutral square club face. A face that will stay square no matter the shaft lean. That square club face depends on a good grip and good turn of the body. The club head must be allowed to feel as though it is rising so that the body can be put in command.

Search out any golf instruction videos, and you'll find at least one influencer touting great iron distance. They then demonstrate from a dead level lie, (probably at a simulator), how advancing the hands results in something like 230 yard (ca. 210 meter) seven irons. This approach is perfectly okay from dead level lies, to a target that isn't raised or downhill. It is especially effective when playing to the longest yardage, not a specific one. On the golf course though, where the lies change, there are hills and valleys, and yardages vary—the necessity to achieve exacting shaft lean becomes a problem.

The issue is pervasive. The shape of your hands has changed, when compared to the gravity fall exercise from chapter one. By allowing the club face to pass square, you have made shaft lean the determining factor in the squareness of the club. Lean the shaft further forward and the club face will open. Lean the shaft backward and the club face will close. *The need to achieve consistent shaft lean is the extraordinary difficulty Hogan overcame.* The best golfer of the 21st century, one of the greatest of all time, found something similar. As evidenced by his ability to hit the ball differing trajectories.

No matter the angle of his shaft, Hogan's club face was always square. The misses golfers have, in their day-to-day rounds, the pushes, pulls, and hooks occur primarily because their hands have moved forward or back as little as an inch. Hogan could be so radical as to descend on the ball with a great deal of shaft lean, then upright the club through impact. In doing so, he would first impart spin, by forcing the ball to climb the face, then regulate trajectory, by causing it to release from the leading edge. That is why he is said to have hit the ball not low or high, neither hitting shots that would bounce and run nor balloon out of control.

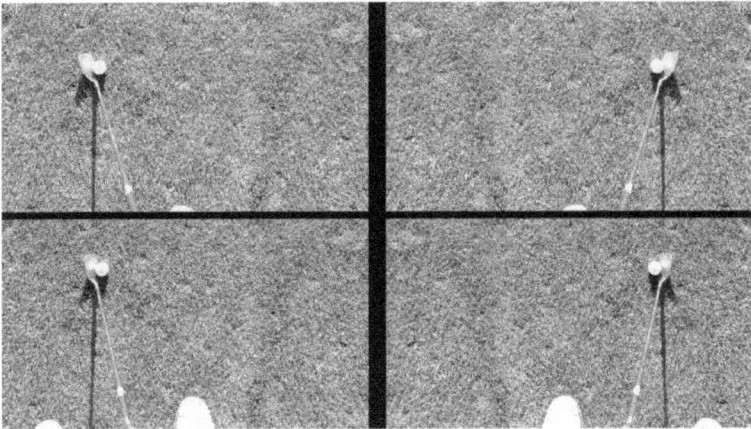

Top and bottom: shafts leaned back wards, in parallel. Top club face remains square. Bottom club closes past square.

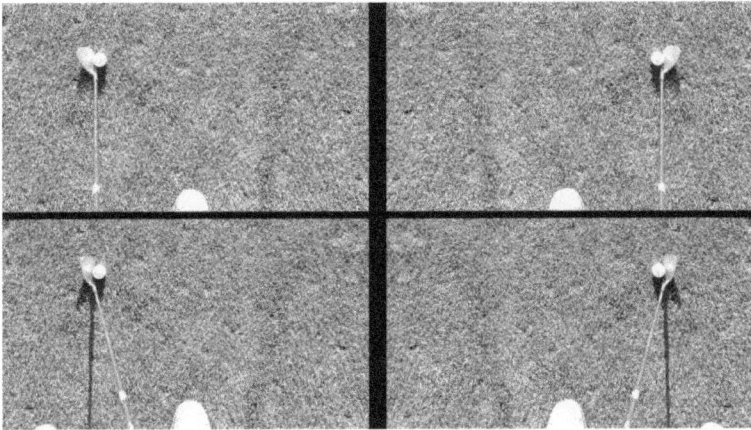

Top: club face remains square even if the shaft has no lean.

No matter what the shaft lean in the above images, from the gravity fall exercise, the club face remains square. That is because your grip is intact. It remains intact through impact because your hands did not force the club to descend. With this ability, you can hit soft shots to greens many feet above and low, boring shots along wooded corridors. You'll be able to predict your distances and select sides of the fairway to play to. Your ability to hit a wedge to a tight pin won't depend on a mixture of slamming the shaft into its advanced position while simultaneously lightening the strike to avoid going long. Instead, you'll be able to apply deft touch with your dominant hand, flighting the ball the necessary trajectory. Without concern over sending it the wrong direction.

Following is the standard address with a three wood. Unlike the wedge, the three wood is moved forward in the stance. This is standardized instruction, not Hogan's methods. Even though the ball is in the position inside the heel Hogan would advocate, the shaft lean problems persist.

Long clubs perform in much the same way as wedges. Here the ball is near the lead heal, per standardized instruction, unlike the middle of the stance, as commonly advised with wedges.

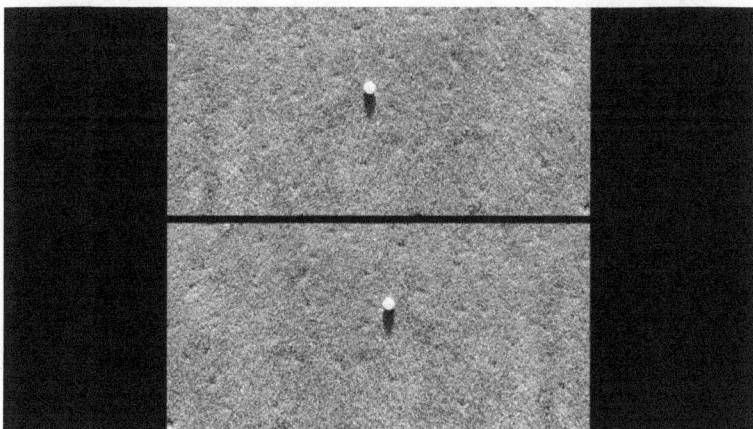

At the top of the back waggle, with the shaft parallel to the stance and target line.

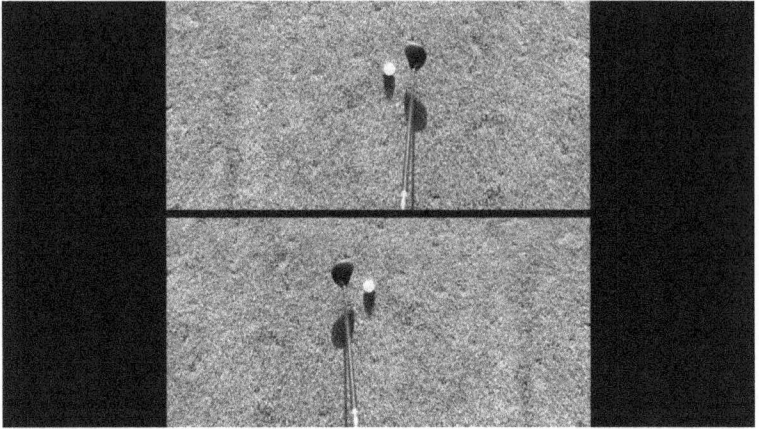

Allowing the club to descend on the ball forces the face shut.

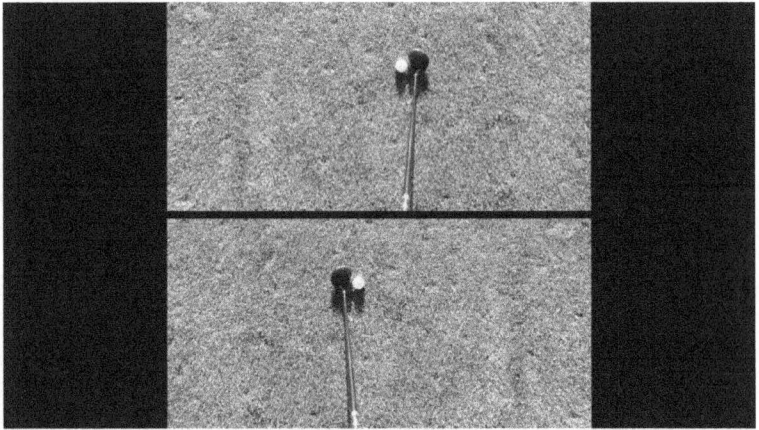

Too little shaft lean results in a pull.

Too much shaft lean results in a push.

Only the just right amount of shaft lean will generate a straight shot.

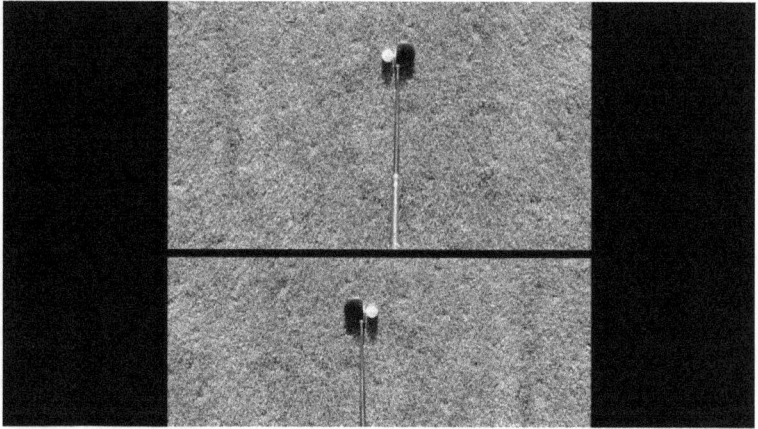

When you resume address, without removing your hands from the club, you'll notice something peculiar. Your hands are on top of the club now. This is also standard golf instruction. Positioning your hands on top of the club is good for hitting the ball further (off line).

In the Hogan swing, the club face rises to square. That is why Hogan advocated for a swing which was below the plane. Then the club would have room to rise. Instead of manipulating the club face open during impact, you're *permitting* the club face to pass square *after* impact. Always in keeping with the pace of your turn.

Hogan advocated for cupping the lead wrist in the back swing, opening the club face wide because it engages his lead hand muscles. ***And also because the club face will never pass square.***

There are tour players who bow their wrists at the top of the swing. They are presetting their shaft lean. If they get it right, they will have success. It is easier to *not rely on precise shaft lean* to hit the ball the right direction.

In the five weeks since I started writing this book, I have made an improvement. This is on schedule. Improvements to your golf swing should occur in three to five week increments. Three weeks to ingrain and two to adopt. Then on to the next element.

The below image lead me to that improvement. Rather than accept that I must hit the ball *high* left-handed, I realized I could establish the trajectory through club head position at the turning point. That realization lead me to a neater understanding of impact.

At the turning point, left-handed my club head is high. At the turning point right-handed my club is low. The left-handed shot went high and the right-handed shot went low.

Next

Your end goal, for using the turning point rehearsal motion, learning to turn on time, is squaring the club no matter your shaft lean, and to waggle as Hogan instructed. Hogan hid all the intentions revealed herein, within his remarkably compact motions. Once you've ingrained the actions necessary to stabilize your club face and turn in sync, you should be able to emulate Hogan's waggle.

Hogan described a waggle of the hands, not the head of the club. All of his instruction revolved around the relationship of the hands and body to the center of the swing. When you execute the waggle outlined on page 67 remember *not to* descend the club to the back of the ball. Merely move your hands forward and feel the club head on its way out and above. Do so while foreseeing the shot.

The benefit of your efforts is the ability to envision the shot, then execute. You should feel electrified, and able to pass your intentions onto the ball. Your mind should not be stuck on impact. The joy of the game is in delivering shots through the air, watching them fly, and land where you deem.

In my experience, emulating the Hogan waggle is easiest at the turning point. How he was able to commune with his shots from the address position is beyond me. Rather than attempt to do as the great man did, you too may find it is easier to assume the Hogan waggle at the turning point position.

Epilogue

Some will do, some will not.

As with all golf instruction, this will stick with some and not with others. I cannot hide the single greatest deterrent to Hogan's success. Not in his tournament golf. His play was exemplary. He went from being very long, during the 1930s, to very consistent, and longish. From 1946 to 1953 his play rivaled the most perfect seasons of any champion. With a 42% win rate. His instruction, on the other hand, was misunderstood. Instructors and students fell away. Now only the most ardent purists pursue Hogan's methods.

The prevailing complaint is a lack of distance. For some time, golfers were told to tuck head covers under their arms. To train them to keep their arms close to their bodies. They were not provided with the tangential information we've discussed. They did not know the explosive strength of bodies separating at a nucleus.

Instead, golfers with head covers tucked under their arms would swing in parallel. Arms and hips flailing at the target. Head covers falling loose or balls being barely struck. They did not see the true error because the instruction was rooted in a lack of understanding.

I won't pretend that *Five Lessons* unlocks your greatest distance. It doesn't. If anything, some players will experience a loss of distance. This loss occurs because flailing creates unrefined club head speed. Almost any visit to an occupied practice tee will reveal golfers lunging for distance.

Hogan's swing from the 30s, compared to later, demonstrates some of these qualities. Extreme arc, to a high-handed, overly long back swing. The kind we see in long drivers of the golf ball. (The kind of swing I too have had.) Then the slash at the bottom and unbalanced unfurling of the hips. Excellent traits for distance, and golf shots which bend inexplicably in either direction. Hogan's miss was a low, screeching hook.

If learning that your playing partner hit less club into a par three is unnerving to you, the instruction from *Five Lessons Distilled* will be difficult to swallow. You're not going to detach your arms from your body just to prove you can hit your five iron further than your buddy. Instead, you're going to hit the right club for the distance within a professional margin—of about eight percent of the original distance—and when your buddy brags they hit less club you'll point out how often they come up short. A flaw which happens more frequently than many golfers like to admit.

You won't have that extra slash distance. Not within the controlled synchronicity of a *Five Lessons* swing. The distilled action will be refined. It will hit the ball consistent distances, with exceptions (manageable misses.) It will also bring consistency to your shot shape.

"Golf is not a game of good shots, it is a game of bad shots." Ben Hogan.

On this topic of distance, trajectory is important to note. For some reason, I foresee high shots. Very, very high shots. Which is why I set up with the club face considerably open, in the neighborhood of fifteen degrees. My ball reaches its apex early and comes down soft. Indeed, only a three wood or driver rolls more than a yard or two into manageable greens.

For those of you who've read Jody Vasquez's book *Afternoons With Mr. Hogan,* this open club face setup will sound familiar. It could be a consequence of age. Although I find that doubtful. When I was young, and working Hogan's Angle into my right-handed swing, I found myself opening the club face considerably at address.

You may foresee lower trajectory windows. For which you can play a square club face. When I square the club face, I feel like I cannot hit the ball the height I want. My trajectory is probably a condition of being a right-hander playing left-handed. Phil Mickelson is in this category. His ball flight is very high as well. I remember hitting low, boring shots right-handed, with absolutely no trepidation. In fact, one of the greatest difficulties, after my injury, was wedges that came out too low.

It's possible I feel the need to hit the ball high because my left hand is not strong enough to deliver those piercing bullets. I certainly cannot throw a football more than 60% as far as I can with my right. I cannot shoot three pointers left-handed, either. The three point line is just too far from the basket.

I can, however, play good golf. By knowing my yardages and hitting my trajectories, with a reliable slight fade.

On the subject of distance, Hogan admitted the very thing that will trouble some golfers. This quality may well be a hitch in golfers willingness to distill their golf swing. That difference is short iron distances. On page 125, along with the ball stance diagram, the text describes a shortening of the arc, regarding short irons. This is due to the open stance. For me, as for Hogan, this opening of the stance is combined with an open club face. We effectively turned our shortest irons into wedges. This is not a bad thing. It is easier to hit a nine iron than a gap wedge. And the majority of shots all of us take are from between 100 and 150 yards (ca. 137 meters). Playing short and mid-irons from those distances is better for our score than hitting pumped up wedges. Especially when we impart spin onto the ball. Flighted balls with spin are easy to control. In the air and upon landing.

Over the past twelve months, I have fully developed the turning point rehearsal motion. I began with the back waggle, then learned to drop the club to the above the ball position. Next, I kept the club moving to inline with my front foot, freeing up my release in the process. I integrated the two-handed basketball pass next. Embracing the true line of the pass to a four to five yard target. Realizing good body rotation in the process, and most recently added the release of the pincer fingers. In those twelve months, I went from an 11.1 handicap to an 8.2, with no end to the drop in sight. I have just now started shooting the kind of scores I hadn't shot since being a twenty-year-old righty.

Relearning the game left-handed meant spending many years comparing my progress. Feeling for so long like I was no better than I had been as a sophomore in high school, after just two years of playing. That was my plateau. I broke that plateau by embracing the turning point motion. All of it is critical, but the most important element is also the strangest, looking off-line behind me. To where my body's momentum needs to go. That directive is indispensable to someone who fights an early extension. Cut that corner and I will go back to flailing early with my hips and back leg. My shots will spray left and short, or worse. I cannot just step up and hit it.

Truthfully, and this is a harsh truth to even the best golfers reading this book. I don't care if you're a winner on the DP, PGA, LPGA, their feeder tours or the LIV tour. Commitment pays off.

Why not rehearse the motion that comes easily when you're playing well?

A note on the early revelations of Hogan's Angle, and its effect on my golf game. In 1998 Annika Sörenstam had spent years playing some of the most dominant golf the LPGA had ever seen. She also did something that made me wonder about Ben Hogan's Secret. She peaked, and I don't mean in golf. Likewise, she peaked with her head. Many of us know that. Early in her down swing, she would look left, at the target. Her head would swivel well before impact. I had been at a plateau at the time. Seldom shooting better than 78, with an eight handicap.

My first attempts revealed something. There was an inside angle that turning revealed. Hitting the ball well, while not looking down, required the dominant arm to locate the ball at a tangent to the target line. Impact had to occur in another place in my mind, at a major deviation from straight. Something else remarkable happened. Repeatable shotmaking. Applying natural force with the dominant arm put the club face in a square position, over and over again.

First, though, that paradigm shift resulted in my first sub 75 average, in competition. As you can tell, I wasn't a naturally gifted golfer. Jack Nicklaus just got it. He was better at twelve or thirteen than I have ever been. Importantly though, like Jack, you and I feel the need to get better. That is why we are here. Conjoined by these words.

The downfall of my newfound understanding was pragmatism. At my playing level, I felt I could become a PGA Professional, and teach and work in golf. Except, how could I teach something that wasn't widely accepted? For anyone who isn't acquainted with the PGA process, there is something called the Player's Ability Test. Essentially, the PGA wants to know that its members can play respectable golf. Thirty-six holes at better than a 76 average, depending on course difficulty, with flat (easy) pin placements. That should have been very achievable for me. After all, tournament golf is played with long punishing rough and difficult pins, in tense situations.

Except, *I could not in good faith use methods that I thought the PGA would reject.*

I also could not play good golf without turning my head, and employing Hogan's Angle. A principle which relied, to my limited understanding, on magical thinking. Having feel, and hitting good golf shots is so difficult, while playing in parallel. I truly don't understand how these delineations have not been made before. After all, Hogan's opening composition, in *Five Lessons*, is a depiction of motors, generators, and synchros operating in tangent.

A word on how I view the drafting of *Five Lessons*. Herbert Warren Wind was an established golf writer. Anthony Ravielli was an illustrator. And Ben Hogan was a golfer with a "secret." Wind wrote from a wealth of knowledge. Ravielli illustrated, as Mr. Hogan directed. And Hogan analyzed freely, to the best of his ability, while maintaining his golf swing. (For a contra example, see the story of Ralph Guldahl. The man for whom the phrase "paralysis by analysis" was coined.)

When I read *Five Lessons,* I get a feeling of unease. Probably because I have better than average drawing skills. The text and the illustrations don't cohere. An illustration will depict something like the two-handed basketball pass, while the text describes hitting the ball. Even just writing that sentence makes me ill. The disconnect is uncanny. Wind operated from prior knowledge, and Ravielli illustrated from instruction. That is why I advise golfers to read *Five Lessons* then reconcile the information, by working from the back of the book to the front, applying only the illustrations and their captions.

I don't mean to disregard Wind's work. I just feel as though the writing should have come after the illustrations, not before, in terms of importance. But then, I have this to write only because that order wasn't taken.

Then again, it's possible the three of them knew exactly what they were doing, and Wind played his part to perfection. After all, Hogan was still competing, and he has expressed his desire to keep the secret out of his competitor's hands. The three of them knew, by concealing the secret as they did, it could only be recovered if someone painstakingly reverse engineered the material.

Millions of people have enjoyed a hallmark of great golf instruction. This author turned the book over and delved in a preordained direction, from back to front. In doing so, he uncovered William Ben Hogan's acclaimed secret.

Addendum

Additional tidbits

The rule of thumb.

We see tour players raise their shaft to their eye line, to align the ball with the target. Ever noticed how they don't always close an eye? If we keep both eyes open while holding the club shaft in front of us, we see two shafts. If the shaft is a consistent distance from our eyes, something interesting happens. We measure a margin.

I call this the rule of thumb because the same exercise can be done with a thumbs up. With our arm outstretched, we know we are repeating the exact distance the thumb is from our eyes. (We look foolish doing this, though.)

However, by holding the shaft up at the same distance from our eyes as our outstretched thumb, we measure a width of approximately eight percent. I.e., if we look through our shaft, at arm's length, to an object 100 yards (ca. 91 meters) away the two shafts will appear to be approximately eight yards apart. Similarly, if we look down the fairway, over a tee shot, we will see shafts at 16 yards (ca. 15 meters) apart at 200 yards (ca. 183 meters) and 20 yards (ca. 18 meters) a part at 250 yards (ca. 229 meters).

We can use this to set markers on either side of the shot. Eight percent represents professional level shotmaking. We then know how much variance we have to hit a professional level shot. Only hitting the ball the right yardage remains.

This trick is especially helpful when playing a new course. We don't know how far away the landing zone is, which can make us uncomfortable. By setting our markers, we establish a reasonable zone width. Which should make us more comfortable with the shot.

The scorecard paints a picture

I call this game mondo mundo. Both mean much.

Ever heard anyone say, "there are no pictures on the scorecard?" Usually regarding a series of bad shots resulting in a good score, by some fluke of luck. Walter Hagen was renowned for hitting one good shot per hole to save his par. What if your scorecard could paint a picture?

Try this accounting procedure the next time you play alone. I think you'll find it helps you stay more engaged. Instead of merely keeping scores or even scores plus greens and fairways, collect dollars for your efforts. They're imaginary dollars, but they help.

Mark the scorecard in this way down the player name column. 1, 20, 10 and score in the top half and 1, 10, 5 and ¢ down the bottom half. The first row 1's represents your tee shots, the next 20s represents shots longer than 150 yards (ca. 137 meters) into the green (these distances can be amended to represent your playing ability), 10s is for shots of less than 150 yards (ca. 137 meters) (this could be less than 100 for instance.) The final row in the top half is of course for score.

In the bottom half, you are accounting for your short game. The 1's column is for feet of putts made. Every first putt is worth a dollar a foot. A missed second putt will cost you a dollar a foot. For instance, if you lag to eight feet and miss the eight footer, (8) will be your entry in that column. Meaning, you must subtract $8. Painful sounding, isn't it? On the flip side, sinking a 20 footer for par will feel—well, like $20.

Next, 10s is a bonus for birdies and 5's is a bonus for pars. This too can be amended to reflect your playing ability. 10's for pars and 5's for bogeys, for instance. So, a 20 footer for par, in the above example, would be good for $20 for the putt and $5 or $10 for the par.

The final row is for chips and pitches. Or the shot taken after a regulation miss. I always give myself cents for this shot. With the number of cents being the same as the club hit. Unless I hole out, in which case I award myself dollars. A chip-in nine iron is good for $9. A chip onto the green with a nine iron is good for 9¢. Putting on is good for 14¢ and holing a bunker shot is worth $15. Hitting the green out of the sand is, of course, good for 15¢. Missing the green with a chip or pitch costs negative cents equal to the club used. Two chipping a green feels rough. The negative cents will amount to the number on the first club plus the number on the second (9 + 12), for instance, for (21) total. May represent a hole where you had to punch out from under a tree, then missed the green with a nine iron and followed up by missing the green with your 56 degree wedge. It will be easy to tell, at a glance, that there was trouble on that hole. Then, if there are no dollars in the putt row the score will add up to a triple bogey. Another example would be missing the green with the first chip (12), for instance, then hitting the green with the second +12, for a total of (0).

The best way to make money is by hitting fairways and greens. Fairways are measured by hitting it in the short grass, even on par threes. The dollars gained equal nineteen (H+1) minus the handicap (N) for the hole. So, on handicap hole #10 the number of dollars earned for hitting the fairway is (N-10) $9. Handicap hole #18 (usually a par three) is good for $1, even for hitting the fairway or the fringe. It is easier to chip or putt from the fringe or fairway, which is why we pay ourselves. Hitting the green on a par three is good for $'s in the 20 or 10 spot, plus the "handi bucks" in the 1's row. So, hitting the green on a 145 yard (ca. 133 meters) par three is good for N-H or 19 - the handicap + $10 for hitting a green from less than 150 yards (ca. 137 meters).

Additionally, laying up successfully on a par five is good for the remainder. E.g., a par five handicapped at #14 is good for $5 off the tee and $14 for the layup. Suddenly, hitting a good layup isn't unimportant anymore. Write the layup dollars in the 20s row. Since your approach had certainly better be from inside 150.

There are numerous benefits to this game. It will help you keep focus on the upcoming shot as well as provide a boost to an otherwise tedious day of solitary golf. It keeps your mind off your score and provides tremendous feedback. Your scorecards will demonstrate how and where you've improved. The greatest benefit is in gaining the ability to put bad shots behind you. Two-chipping a hole only costs negative cents. Even if it results in a double bogey. The twenty plus dollars that can result from hitting the green on the next par three will certainly offset that.

Another negative amount is penalty shots. They certainly do hurt. As they should. Instead of dollars in the "handi bucks" row, you get negative dollars for hitting it out of bounds, or in the water. Instead of 10s or 20s for hitting the green, you lose 10s or 20s for hitting it in the drink. That'll teach you. Losing a ball is truly miserable. Bounce back, though. Hitting the fairway after losing money cancels the loss. That's the only way to play. A negative in the "handi bucks" row followed with a big slash through the negative. Take that lost ball. You rebounded. Sure, the score will reflect the penalty. The money will feel right, though. That's how golf should be. A measure of our ability to bounce back.

This is the method I use to appraise a golfer's progress. So much focus in golf is on the golf swing. The greater question is the golfer's game.

Hopeful professionals, use this tool to measure your ability to play for cash. That distinction will affect your game. Can you consistently generate enough imaginary money to live on? Does knowing a shot is worth dollars positively or negatively influence your feelings about that shot?

Tweak the dollar amounts to fit your lifestyle. A ten dollar bill may mean little to you. Up the ante. A general rule of thumb is a good round should pay 4x more than the green fee cost. Green fees where I live range between $35 and $60. That is why a round of 85 is worth about $200. For most golfers, 85 is a respectable score.

Example:

HDCP	10	2	14	6	12	18	16	4	8	
1			13	7	1	3	15			39
20	10				18		$			48
10	$		($)		$	$				20
5	6	4	6	4	4	4	5	4	41	
PAR	5	4	4	3	4	5	3	4	4	36
1	(10)	6			12		(8)	3		3
10					$					10
5		$		$			$			15
¢	14	11	8		7	10				.50

135.50

This example shows how the golfer could be on track to breaking 80 simply by eliminating three putts. They had just one up and down but put together a good string of fairways and made decent money.

White	1	2	3	4	5	6	7	8	9		
HDCP	10	2	14	6	12	18	16	4	8		
1			13	7	1	3	15				39
20	10					$					30
10	$		(1)	$	3						20
8	6	5	64	4	4	4	54	42			
PAR	5	4	4	3	4	5	3	4	4	36	
1	(10)				12	(8)	3				(3)
10					$						10
5				$			$				10
¢		14	11	8		7	10				.50

$106.50

This is the same card, only without the up and down on #2 and successful layup on the par five 6th. The stroke difference is only one. However, the dollar total shows the misses.

White	1	2	3	4	5	6	7	8	9	
HDCP	10	2	14	6	12	18	16	4	8	
1			13	7	1	3	15			39
20	10					16	8			46
10	8		8		8	8				40
8	6	3	44	44	4	4	54	38		
PAR	5	4	4	3	4	5	3	4	4	36
1	(10)				12	(8)	3			(3)
10					8					10
5			8	8			8			15
¢	$14		8			7	10			14.25

$161.25

With some improvement, this golfer could eliminate the penalty on #3 and enjoy chip-in on #2. Plus add back in the good layup on the par five. In doing so, his dollar tally would look more invigorating.

I once kept track of a 67 Rory McIlroy shot at The Masters and he came in at over $500. On Saturday I hit 12 of 18 greens and 7 of 13 fairways en route to four over par 75 worth $355.61. Much of that money was made because I'm a short hitter who has to lay up on almost every par 5, and regularly plays approaches from outside 150 yards. Although, playing short irons from that 110 to 140 yard range was good for $91. They're just so easy to hit. The 33 putts it took most certainly could be better. However, I'll know I've improved when my payout exceeds $400. At the beginning of the season I had $90 rounds. So learning to turn on time, keern, my golf swing rehearsal has certainly been beneficial.

This is my number (406)393-9019. This number is only for golfers. Reach me there, or by email to hogansangle@gmail.com. I see my buddies playing better golf, getting out of slumps, and winning tournaments. I don't do much. I play my game, and talk to them about what they're doing. It takes me a long time to figure anything out. So most of that talk is just me making sure I understand what they're saying. I like people and I like golf. I like to hear about people's feels, and what they're working on. I don't have time to be everyone's friend.

Which is where mondo mundo comes in. Say I had come to myself at the beginning of the season and said, "I'm not even earning $100 a round. I should be doing a lot better."

I would take a look at my game and say, "where do you want to be?"

If I said, "$300 a round."

I would take a look at my game to see if I thought I could get there. Then I would say, "when?"

"September."

"Okay, that's six months from now, you just earned $96 today. So, spread $204 over the next six months. We'll see if we can get you there."

As it turns out, I managed, and then some. What did I get for my hypothetical $204? I got the contents of a book. I knew this year was about setting new standards. Last year, I broke down my old swing. I built a device for that. You can see it on my YouTube channel: Hogan'sAngle. This year, I set about improving, with a much better swing. I was determined to have a paradigm shift. Now, on bad days, windy brutal days, I shoot the kind of scores that satisfied me one year ago.

So, let's say you want to get better. This is what that would look like. You message me a picture of a scorecard. We talk. I break down the dollar value of the round. Then you tell me where you want to be and how long you want it to take. I consider whether I can get you there, or not. Then we spread the difference over the time.

You're shooting $150 rounds. You want to be shooting $250 rounds by the Member Guest, which is in two months. Okay, that's $50 a month. Let's talk.

For your money you get someone to communicate with. Maybe we play. Maybe we practice. I'm not the kind of person who is going to stand on the range, speaking advice into your ear, touching your hands to move them into a different position. I'm also not big on heavy swing analysis. Your swing isn't' meant to fit into a perfect swing mold. Sorry, that's just not the case. Not for anyone. We work with what you've got, and flex and stretch, and recognize that things are going to change.

I know Hogan because Hogan isn't arbitrary. His work also isn't superficial. Even though people covet his swing, he put function over form. Sure, a well functioning swing looks better. The point is to build a swing that looks like it's yours. Like it belongs to you.

I've had to do so much more to become good at golfing left-handed that I have patience for imperfection. I'll listen to what you're doing and consider what next steps may be. I communicate with drawings and questions. I prefer that you arrive at your own conclusions.

I'll expect you to keep track of your rounds. I want to know what you're shooting. I want to know how things are working out. Periodically, I'll ask you to plan a test day. That may involve an otherwise simple round with your buddies. Maybe I'll play too. I like to play golf. That day should feel like competition.

You're competing to save yourself money. There should be nerves. That's the kind of thing that helps a person grow.

During that round, you'll be setting a new dollar amount. We'll go over your scorecard again, and I'll tally your figure. Maybe you'll meet your goal, and you'll say to me, "thanks, I did it. I got there." If you're ahead of schedule, we'll forgive the remainder of our arrangement. Or, maybe you'll say, "that was good but I can do better. Let's set a new goal."

The new goal may mean stretching the same monthly amount over a longer time. Or it may involve upping the figure. Your game, your goals. In exchange for your payments you have someone to keep you on task.

That someone (me) also values their time. So, a basic rule of thumb is, for every dollar you spend you get two minutes of my time. Send me a simple text, get a simple response, that's good for a minute. (I don't count time I spend playing my game against you. If I've got the time to play golf I'm a happy man.) Send me weekly updates with no expectation of a response, then call me up and talk my ear off for thirty minutes. That could be just what you need. As long we're making good use of our time, we're going to make progress.

I don't remember the professional golfer, off the top of my head, but he was playing with Mr. Hogan. Ben hit a burner two iron just over a green side bunker and it stopped close to the pin. The golfer ran across the fairway and handed him his card, "Ben, if Valerie doesn't want to hear about that shot, give me a call!"

I can identify with that guy. It doesn't have to be a burner two iron though, or any particular shot at all. I'll take what you tell me and think about it. Then I'll come up with ideas. Like I said, I see my closest golfing buddies getting over slumps and shooting personal bests. I like their personal growth. I want to see more. I just don't have *free* time for everyone.

(406)393-9019. I'm listed online under Hogan's Angle. The guys at the golf courses where I live know that I'm not the kind of person to hone in on their lessons, by crowding their practice tee, pounding advice into people's ears. If that's the kind of lesson you want, I'm sure you can find someone. It won't be me.

This methodology, not just uncovering Hogan's Secret, but figuring out a way to share that I'm comfortable with, has taken a long time. I hope to be able to balance my love of the game, with my love of your game. And when I need a break I'll put my boat on the water.

About the author

K. Zachary Haslem "Keern" lives alternately in Montana and Nevada. He also writes stage plays, screen plays and directs television and film. For fun, he sails his beloved self-made proa, Huck Luna, (a pacific island outrigger canoe) every chance he gets. His favorite voyage being the wild stretch of the mighty Missouri River. He owes his willingness to publicize what would otherwise be a private, pleasurable outlet, his work in golf, to having found a suitable pastime. Working on and sailing his boat.